Straight Talk About...
DIGITAL DANGERS

Rachel Stuckey

Crabtree Publishing Company
www.crabtreebooks.com

Straight Talk About...

Produced for Crabtree Publishing by:
Infinch Solutions

Publishing Director: Ravi Lakhina

Author: Rachel Stuckey

Project Controller: Vishal Obroi

Editors: John Perritano, Rebecca Sjonger

Proofreader: Shannon Welbourn

Art director: Dibakar Acharjee

Designer: Rajbir

Project coordinator: Kelly Spence

Production coordinator: Margaret Amy Salter

Prepress technician: Margaret Amy Salter

Consultant: Jessica Alcock, Residential Counselor BA Psychology, MA Child and Youth Studies

Photographs:
Cover: Sylvie Bouchard/Shutterstock Inc.
Title page: BrianWancho/Shutterstock Inc.; p.4: Warren Goldswain/Shutterstock Inc.; p.6: SpeedKingz/Shutterstock Inc.; p.8: Monkey Business Images/Shutterstock Inc.; p.11: oliveromg/Shutterstock Inc.; p.12: MJTH/Shutterstock Inc.; p.14: vita khorzhevska/Shutterstock Inc.; p.16: scyther5/Shutterstock Inc.; p.17: Pressmaster/Shutterstock Inc.; p.18: arek_malang/Shutterstock Inc.; p.20: Ruslan Everst/Shutterstock Inc.; p.21: Bloomua/Shutterstock Inc.; p.24: oliveromg/Shutterstock Inc.; p.27: Bloomua/Shutterstock Inc.; p.28: Iakov Filimonov/Shutterstock Inc.; p.29: Cheryl Savan/Shutterstock Inc.; p.30: Photographee.eu/Shutterstock Inc.; p.32: Feng Yu/Shutterstock Inc.; p.33: Ingvar Bjork/Shutterstock Inc.; p.34: Twin Design/Shutterstock Inc.; p.37: scyther5/Shutterstock inc.; p.38: Monkey Business Images/Shutterstock Inc.; p.41: Bloomua/Shutterstock Inc. p.42: Monkey Business Images/Shutterstock Inc.

Library and Archives Canada Cataloguing in Publication

Stuckey, Rachel, author
    Digital dangers / Rachel Stuckey.

(Straight talk about...)
Includes index.
Issued in print and electronic formats.
ISBN 978-0-7787-2202-1 (bound).--ISBN 978-0-7787-2206-9 (pbk.).--ISBN 978-1-4271-9977-5 (pdf).--ISBN 978-1-4271-9973-7 (html)

    1. Computer crimes--Juvenile literature. 2. Cyberbullying--Juvenile literature. 3. Online sexual predators--Juvenile literature.
4. Internet--Security measures--Juvenile literature. I. Title.
II. Series: Straight talk about...

HV6773.S78 2015   j364.16'8   C2014-908099-9
                                            C2014-908100-6

Library of Congress Cataloging-in-Publication Data

Stuckey, Rachel.
  Digital dangers / Rachel Stuckey.
      pages cm. -- (Straight talk about...)
  Includes index.
  ISBN 978-0-7787-2202-1 (reinforced library binding) --
ISBN 978-0-7787-2206-9 (pbk.) --
ISBN 978-1-4271-9977-5 (electronic pdf) --
ISBN 978-1-4271-9973-7 (electronic html)
  1. Internet and children--Safety measures--Juvenile literature.
2. Cyberbullying--Prevention--Juvenile literature. 3. Privacy, Right of--Juvenile literature. 4. Online social networks--Security measures--Juvenile literature. 5. Social media--Juvenile literature. I. Title.

  HQ784.I58S78 2015
  302.34'302854678--dc23
                                            2014045076

Crabtree Publishing Company

www.crabtreebooks.com   1-800-387-7650

Printed in Canada/022015/MA20150101

Published in Canada
Crabtree Publishing
616 Welland Ave.
St. Catharines, ON
L2M 5V6

Published in the United States
Crabtree Publishing
PMB 59051
350 Fifth Avenue, 59th Floor
New York, NY 10118

Published in the United Kingdom
Crabtree Publishing
Maritime House
Basin Road North, Hove
BN41 1WR

Published in Australia
Crabtree Publishing
3 Charles Street
Coburg North
VIC, 3058

CONTENTS

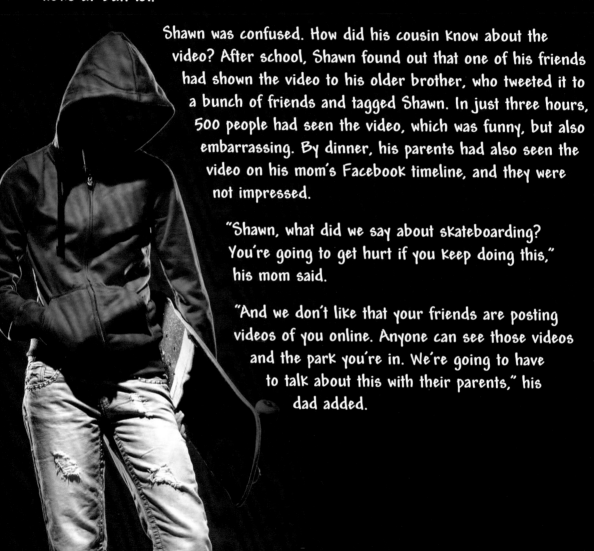

Shawn got a text just before he sat down to eat breakfast. His friend had posted a video on YouTube of them falling off their skateboards. Shawn laughed and then forwarded the link to some of his other buddies.

At lunch, his cousin who lived in another city sent him a text: "dude cool vid hows ur butt lol."

Shawn was confused. How did his cousin know about the video? After school, Shawn found out that one of his friends had shown the video to his older brother, who tweeted it to a bunch of friends and tagged Shawn. In just three hours, 500 people had seen the video, which was funny, but also embarrassing. By dinner, his parents had also seen the video on his mom's Facebook timeline, and they were not impressed.

"Shawn, what did we say about skateboarding? You're going to get hurt if you keep doing this," his mom said.

"And we don't like that your friends are posting videos of you online. Anyone can see those videos and the park you're in. We're going to have to talk about this with their parents," his dad added.

Introduction
A Bad Situation

Shawn learned the hard way that life in the digital world is fast. What he thought was a private joke became public in a few short hours. Smartphones, email, and social networking sites are common and may seem harmless. However, dangers lurk behind every text, every keystroke, and every tweet.

Cyber bullying and online predators are just a couple of digital dangers. Other things that might make you uncomfortable include seeing material meant for adults or feeling pressure to sext.

The Internet is a minefield of phishers, malware, and hackers. Thinking before you post and protecting your privacy are the first steps to creating a positive digital experience. When you're online you need to be smart and safe.

"This one girl at school used to send me mean text messages. I ignored her, but things kept getting worse. Finally, I got mad and posted a rumor about her on Twitter. A few weeks later, someone took a video of me changing in the girls' locker room and posted it on a fake profile. Everyone in my school saw it." Amelia, aged 15.

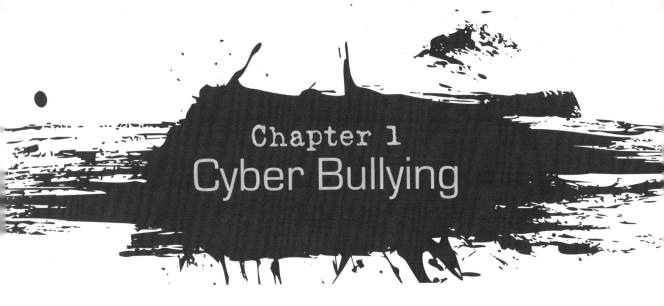

Chapter 1
Cyber Bullying

Bullies no longer just prowl school hallways, playgrounds, or malls. They also torment people in the digital world where everyone has a front-row seat. This is called cyber bullying. Cyber bullying is any type of **harassment** that happens through digital communication.

Cyber bullies use social networking sites, video sharing, blogs, email, instant messages, chat applications, or texting. Cyber bullies can send mean texts or emails, or post hurtful things that others can see. They can create fake profiles and websites.

Boys and girls can both be bullies, whether it's in person or in cyberspace. Researchers have found that girls are just as likely to engage in cyber bullying as boys.

A Wide Audience

Cyber bullies can reach many people quickly. Bullying in the digital world is often hard for adults to see if they're not aware of the online habits of younger people who have grown up with technology. Moreover, cyber bullying can happen behind the victim's back, who may not understand why people are laughing at him or her.

Cyber bullying may be the most dangerous type of harassment. The pictures and words used to cyber bully never go away. In addition, cyber bullying often leads to other kinds of bullying, such as verbal or physical. Bullies often remain **anonymous**—no one knows them by their real names. People who read a bully's texts or see his or her photos may think of these acts of bullying as entertainment.

Being cyber bullied can be an emotionally traumatic experience.

Bullying with a Digital Twist

Cyber bullying is a type of social bullying. Social bullies try to harm a person's reputation or relationships with others. Cyber bullying adds a digital twist. Here are some examples of cyber bullying:

- sending or posting hurtful messages over email, text, or social media
- posting lies or private information
- posting or sending embarrassing information or photographs to others
- getting other people to post or send hurtful messages
- encouraging others to exclude someone from an online group
- damaging someone's social reputation or sense of belonging
- **impersonating,** or pretending to be someone else
- using a person's password to access his or her social profile or email
- creating websites designed to humiliate or embarrass someone

Amanda's Story

The story of Amanda Todd is an extreme example of the dangers of cyber bullying. In the seventh grade, someone convinced Amanda to take off her shirt during a web cam chat. The unknown man took a **screenshot**, or picture of the image, on his computer of her topless. He sent it to her friends online and used the image in a fake Facebook account that he set up using Amanda's name.

Amanda had no way to stop her schoolmates and others from seeing the image. After years of humiliation and bullying at school and online, she posted a video telling her story. Suddenly, complete strangers started to harass her online. Even though thousands of people around the world offered support, the cyber bullying was too much for fifteen-year-old Amanda. A few weeks later, she committed suicide.

By the Numbers

- About one in four young people have engaged in some form of digital harassment.
- In a 2008 study, two-thirds of students who reported being bullied in the previous three months were targeted using instant messaging or email.
- According to a 2009 report, more than 80 percent of young people think cyber bullying is easier to get away with than bullying someone in person.
- Some estimates suggest only one in 10 victims will tell an adult about cyber bullying.

Source: Dosomething.org; Bullyingstatistics.org; University of Toronto

Make a Difference

A **bystander** is any person who witnesses an action or an event but is not involved. Because cyber bullying happens online, the number of bystanders is almost limitless. When bystanders spread gossip, nasty messages, or embarrassing photos, they become bullies, too.

You and your friends may not realize how dangerous it is to gossip online. Thinking before you act, refusing to participate, or offering support to a victim can make a huge difference. Most importantly, you can report cyber bullying to a responsible adult.

Cyber bullying can hurt just as much as traditional bullying.

"This guy kept liking my Instagram posts, saying I was really talented. I started following him on Twitter and he seemed cool. I gave him my Kik and we started chatting a lot about art. Then he started asking me weird questions. He asked me to send him pictures of myself. It was creepy. I told my sister and she told me to block him." Erik, aged 16.

Chapter 2
Liars and Predators

Some people want to hunt down and hurt others. They are predators. The chances that you will encounter a predator on the street, at a park, or at school are very low. In the digital world, however, predators can easily find you.

Have you ever started chatting online with someone who likes all the same things you do? The same movies? The same music? The same teams? He or she always seems to be interested in what you have to say.

If you have a fight with your best friend, your online friend will take your side. He or she flatters you and makes you feel good about yourself. This person might even send you gifts or money. Sounds like a perfect friend, right? It also sounds like an online predator.

New Best Friend?

Becoming a person's digital best friend is how an online predator earns trust. Predators are smart. They understand how young people feel. They know the different types of relationship problems kids have.

Predators are on the lookout for anyone going through a tough time. People at risk include kids whose parents fight, those who have recently lost a friend, or those who are struggling through other difficult times.

Whether you're at the park, at school, or online, be careful of predators.

Sexual Predators

Some online predators are **pedophiles**, adults who are sexually attracted to children. Pedophiles often use digital devices and material to look at **child pornography** and share it with other predators. Some pedophiles try to convince young people to meet them in person and begin an adult relationship. They may also send unwanted messages or pornographic images.

14

What is Pornography?

Pornography includes text, images, and videos that describe or show sexual acts. Pornography is something that some adults enjoy and others do not.

Sometimes artists take photos of naked people or make movies about adult relationships. Such things are not pornography. They are works of art. Pornography is just about sex.

However, in most places, police consider any **sexually explicit** material involving children or teenagers under 18 to be child pornography. It is against the law to make it, share it, or even have it on your phone or computer.

Don't Delete!

If you get sexually explicit material in an email or text, don't delete it. Tell an adult you trust right away. If someone makes you uncomfortable online, do not delete what that person sent you. Tell an adult so he or she can call the police.

Sometimes you might stumble upon material that is meant for adults. You should still tell an adult about what you saw and where. You can talk about how it made you feel and how to prevent seeing it again.

Phishers and Catfish

Not all online predators are interested in sex. Some are trying to steal money. They try to get people to share passwords, personal information, credit card numbers, and bank account details. This is called **phishing**. Once they get this information, phishers pretend to be someone else to buy things or steal money.

Liars abound in the digital world. Some people create online fantasies and pretend to be other people. These people, known as **catfish**, seek friendships and romantic relationships using their fake identities.

Phishers try to steal credit information.

Some people who seek help or sympathy online might not actually need it.

Attention-Seeking Behavior

People may lie to get attention online. Some will make up horrible, sad stories about their lives. They may pretend to have a sick child or be a victim of a crime. They try to make friends with the people who show them support, never telling the truth about their lives.

Some people pretend to have a deadly disease. They create websites or blogs and send emails. Some want money. Others want attention. One real cancer patient in Seattle, Washington, wrote a popular blog about her struggle with cancer. Through her blog, she encountered at least three women who pretended to also have cancer. The real cancer patient felt sorry for those pretending to be sick just to gather attention.

"This kid in my class found a picture of a dog on Flickr and put the principal's face on it. Then she posted it on Facebook. It was funny, and everybody was making comments. Someone's mom told the principal. Everybody that commented on the photo got in trouble and the girl was suspended for a long time."
Brad, aged 16.

Chapter 3
Social Media

Social media and social networking are amazing. They connect people all over the world and have changed the way we share information. Facebook is the most popular social media network with more than one billion users.

Many kids avoid using Facebook because their parents and teachers use it. They would rather not share information with adults. Instead, kids are using new social media apps without understanding the sometimes dangerous consequences of doing so.

Young people must be aware of the risks of social media so they can help protect themselves. Keeping important information private, deleting content, being anonymous, and not revealing your location are all concerns to keep in mind when it comes to social media.

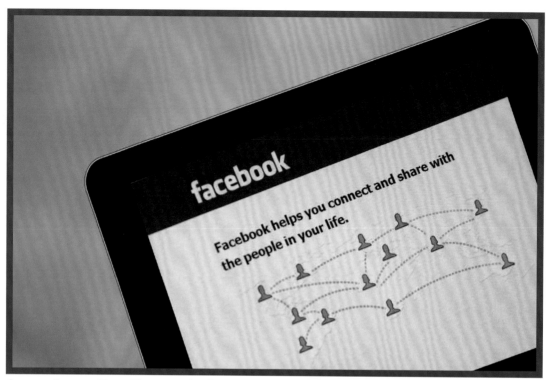

According to Pew Research, 94 percent of teens have an average of 425 Facebook "friends."

The Biggest Book in the World

It seems like everyone has a Facebook page. Most people use their own names and photos so that other users will recognize them. Other people set up fake profiles or lie about their names, their ages, where they live, or what they look like.

Facebook is always updating the way it protects users' privacy. Still, it's important to check your privacy settings, too. When you comment on a photo or post that is public, everyone on Facebook can see it. If you don't set your profile to "friends only," everyone on Facebook can see your information.

Think Before You Tweet

Twitter is a more public type of social media than Facebook. Users post short "tweets" that can include links to photos, videos, and websites. The entire world can see what you post, unless you set your **feed** to private.

Twitter users can also "retweet" your posts—increasing the number of people who see your original tweet. Retweeting can also be dangerous. If you post where you live or where you go to school, any user can see it. A popular blogger in Arizona once tweeted about being on vacation and a burglar broke into his house while he was away!

Each tweet can use a maximum of 140 characters.

Instant Photos

Instagram is a way to share photos, as are Facebook and Twitter. Instagram, however, is public. Your photos are **geotagged**, which means people can see where you are when you take them. Predators can use this information to find potential targets. It's important to change your settings on Instagram to protect your privacy.

Safety Tips for Social Media

- Avoid publishing personal information.
- Pick a username that does not include your age, where you live, or where you go to school.
- Remember that what you post online can never really be deleted.
- Never post comments that are abusive or inappropriate.
- Use the privacy features so only your friends can see your profile or feed.
- Be careful about who you allow to join your network and watch out for fake profiles.

Online = $$$

In 2011, an eight-year-old girl spent her winter break playing a game on her family's iPad. She didn't understand that the prizes she collected in the game cost real money. Her mom's credit card was charged $1,400.

Since that incident, Apple, the company that makes the iPad, has added extra steps so that users have to confirm purchases made within an app before they make them. Still, it's possible to **download** hundreds of dollars of content if you don't pay attention to what you are buying.

By the Numbers

- According to a 2014 study by KnowTheNet.Org, almost 60 percent of children had used a social media site before they were 10 years old.
- More than half of all young people ignore Facebook's age limit of 13 years.
- More than 40 percent of young people have messaged strangers on social media sites.
- Other surveys show that 50 percent of teenagers log into a social media site every day.

Source: KnowTheNet.Org

"One day I was online when an instant message popped up on my cell. It was some strange guy who called himself chad76. I didn't know who he was. He wanted to know what my name was, what I was doing, and what I was wearing. Ewwwww, I said to myself. Then I blocked him." Shelby, aged 14.

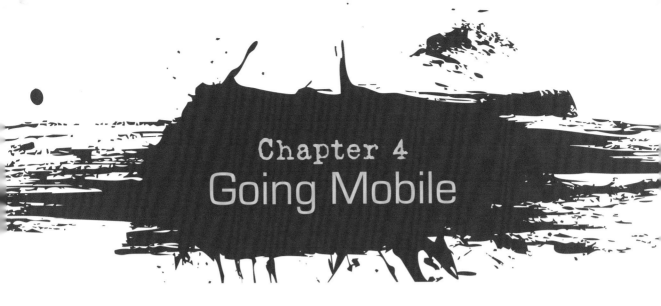

Chapter 4
Going Mobile

Sending texts and chatting over instant message apps are two of the most popular forms of digital communication. Smartphones with screens and keyboards allow us to send messages quickly and easily from almost anywhere. Smartphones also connect to the Internet, making them portable computers. Moreover, many people use tablets to connect to phone networks. Although going mobile is fun, just like regular computers, you have to take certain steps to remain safe.

Instant Communication

Texting and instant messaging are fast ways to communicate. There are many instant messaging apps, with more being created each year. It's difficult to keep track of them all! Many people use their own names when they create their chat **handles**. However, there's no way to know for certain with whom you're really chatting.

What is Sexting?

Sexting is using texts or instant messages to send sexually explicit messages, images, or videos to another person. Sexting often happens when flirting with a boy or girl on a cell phone goes too far. Sexting is very risky.

What you thought was private might become public. Cyber bullies can use your sext messages against you. Moreover, naked or sexually explicit pictures of an underage person on your phone or computer might be considered child pornography.

No Name is No Good

Many instant message apps, such as Kik, can be completely anonymous. Kik users do not have to use their full names or phone numbers. They can also chat on tablets. This app is very popular with teenagers because they can hide their conversations from adults. Still, using this type of app can be dangerous because you never know with whom you're really chatting.

Forget-Me-Not

Most instant messaging apps save conversation histories, which means what you send and receive is logged online forever. Sometimes that's a good thing. Other times we send messages we regret later. Even if someone deletes your message, it still exists somewhere on the Internet.

When you press "send," you can't take it back.

Nothing Disappears in a Snap

Snapchat combines instant messaging with images. When you send a photo to someone on Snapchat, the app deletes the image on both your phones after 10 seconds. Snapchat makes sending private or embarrassing images seem easier or safer. Beware! The person who gets the photo can take a screenshot of anything on his or her device before the image is deleted.

Where Are You?

Smartphones and other mobile devices have Global Positioning System (GPS) locators that always know where your mobile device is. Moreover, many smartphone apps use GPS to tell users where others are located. While this can make it easy for adults to meet, it is a minefield for young people. Apps that use GPS make it easy for online predators to locate potential targets.

For example, Yik Yak shares posts with the 500 nearest users. That means the people who read your post know you are nearby. The Whisper app also allows users to see which areas the posts came from.

GPS systems are great ways for you to figure out where you're going, but predators can also use them to find you.

Be careful of what you pay for with your cell phone. The bills can rack up.

Nothing's Free

Accessing the Internet from mobile devices isn't free. Companies charge to use their digital networks. It is very important that you pay attention to the limits of your account. If you don't pay attention to your bill, you might owe your cell phone carrier or Internet provider a lot of money.

Even if you have an unlimited data plan, there may be hidden costs. For example, ring tones and other downloads often have extra charges. International texts and phone calls may not be included in your plan.

"I once got an email that was from Facebook. It said that my friend had posted something on my wall. When I clicked on the link in the email, it asked me for my password. Later I found out that my Facebook account was totally hacked and all my friends got the same messages. I changed my password after that." Maria, aged 16.

Chapter 5
The Online World

The Internet can be a very fun and informative place. Without the Internet, there would be no websites and no email.

It's important to be **cyber literate**, though. This means being knowledgeable about the risks of the online world. You must be critical and use good judgment about information you find online.

Anyone can use the Internet to create websites and send emails. The Internet makes it easy to create and send videos, or to steal someone else's hard work and say it's your own.

In a digital world, you always have to question if something is real or true. You can't believe everything you read or see. You have to check and then check again. Even reputable sites can get it wrong.

Email

People use email to send thank-you letters to grandparents, assignments to teachers, and job applications to potential employers. It's faster, easier, and cheaper than regular mail.

Spam is a type of email sent to strangers. Here's how spam works: a person creates a computer robot to look for email addresses online and sends messages to each one. Some spam emails contain **computer viruses**, while others send ads for various products and services. Most email **programs** filter out spam as junk mail, but they don't always work. Never open spam messages—doing so sends a signal to the robot to send you more.

Hoaxes are another type of email danger. These emails often tell amazing stories that are not true. Still, some people believe them and the email is forwarded from person to person.

Everyone receives spam. Just be careful which messages you open.

Is This for Real?

Not all the information on the Internet is true. To help you choose what to believe, ask these questions:

- What is the purpose of this website?
- Who owns or who made this website?
- Who wrote this information? If a source doesn't tell you who they are, never trust the information.

Companies trying to sell products may not always tell you the entire story. People with strong opinions may ignore important facts. It is easy for anyone to build a website and post false information.

Wiki What?

Wikipedia is an online source for general knowledge. Volunteers write and edit the entries found on this website. Sometimes, though, they miss false information. To make sure the article is accurate, check the sources that Wikipedia uses. The website lists them at the bottom of the page. If you have doubts, search for other sources you can trust. Just because it is on Wikipedia doesn't mean it's accurate or true.

Wikipedia is a popular site to find general information, but don't assume all that information is true.

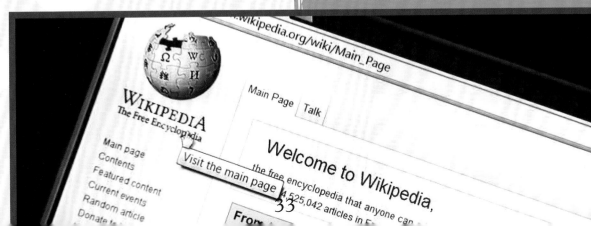

33

Watch This!

Videos are a great way to tell stories. There are many video-sharing sites on the Internet. YouTube is one of the most widely used. Other sites like Vimeo are popular with artists and creative people. Vine is a video-sharing site that lets anyone create short **looping**, or repeating, videos. Upworthy is a site that gathers videos with positive messages from the Internet.

A video may not tell the whole story, though. You can't always be sure that what you're viewing is actually what happened. Videos only show a small part of an event from one perspective. They can also be edited or changed.

Videos can be edited and changed, so be wary of what you watch.

YouTube

YouTube is home to many different types of videos that people make and **upload**. Uploading is putting videos or pictures from your phone or computer on to the Internet. Some videos are clips from movies and TV shows. Others are music videos. Short comedy videos or "how to" videos are also very popular.

YouTubers—or YouTube stars—have many fans and can make a lot of money. "Superwoman," for example, has four million subscribers. She is paid every time a viewer watches an advertisement on her channel.

Often people will use their phone cameras to record events and then post the videos on YouTube. It's a good idea to be careful about what you do or say in another person's video. You just might find yourself an unwilling star on YouTube.

By the Numbers

- People upload more than 100 hours of video to YouTube every minute.
- Every month, more than one billion people visit YouTube.
- One out of every three young people watches online videos more than TV.

Source: YouTube

Follow the Rules

YouTube has rules about what can and cannot be uploaded to the site. For example, YouTube won't allow people to upload sexually explicit videos. They also have rules on how people who comment should behave. YouTube includes a safety option that will put a filter on inappropriate content.

Trolling for Comments

Have you ever read the comments section of a YouTube video, a news site, or a blog? People want you to comment on what they post. They want to engage with their readers or viewers. A blogger will often pose a question at the end of his or her posts to encourage readers to comment.

The comments section of any site is also where angry people can voice their frustrations. They often write nasty comments. **Trolls** are people who make negative comments on purpose to start fights with other readers. **Moderators**, or the people who control what happens on websites, protect users against trolls by removing offensive messages.

Commenting with Facebook

Facebook is the only way to comment on some websites, making it impossible for people to leave anonymous comments. If you comment on another website using Facebook, your comments will show up on your own **wall**.

Commenting on websites is a great way to make your opinion known—just be considerate.

Sexism on the Net

Sexism is treating people unfairly based on whether they are male or female. It's common to see sexist, rude, or hateful comments about women by men on websites. Sometimes when a woman expresses an opinion or demonstrates her knowledge of a topic in a YouTube video, some people will comment on the shape of the woman's body or say rude things about her.

Fourteen-year-old Simon started playing the video
game World of Warcraft during his first semester
of high school. It was very hard for him to stop
playing. He played so much that he neglected his
homework. When Simon came home with his first
report card, his parents were surprised to learn
their son was failing three of his classes and just
barely passing the others.

Chapter 6
Gaming

People often think video games are played mainly by boys but girls now make up about half of all gamers. Whether on a laptop, tablet, or smartphone, video games can be a fun way to relax or spend time with friends.

Nevertheless, video games have a bad reputation. Many games, such as *Grand Theft Auto, Call of Duty,* and *Dead or Alive,* include lifelike violence and negative images of women. Research suggests that about 90 percent of the games played by children contain adult content.

Video games can be **addictive**. Addicted players are unable to stop playing when it's time to do other things, such as eating a meal, doing homework, or going to class. Addicts may lie and cheat to play more. Some extreme gamers hurt their bodies from playing too much. One gamer in South Korea died in 2005 after playing *Starcraft* for days. He didn't eat or sleep enough and passed away from heart failure.

Dangers of Gaming

The content of games and the amount of time you play are the most obvious issues that concern parents. They often overlook other dangers. Video games are a type of social media—players connect with other players online. You're more likely to connect with a stranger in a game than on other forms of social media.

It's normal, and even fun, to "trash talk" your opponent. Such comments can turn into cyber bullying very easily. Remember that every player is in control of his or her own game. You can kick a player out of your game or walk away at any time. If another player makes you uncomfortable, tell an adult. The Pew Internet & American Life Project reports that half of teens who play online video games experienced other players being mean or overly aggressive.

What's in a Name--or a Face?

When playing online games, it's best to make up a game handle and not use your real name. Your handle should be different from any other online profiles you might have, and it should not include any personal details, such as your address or telephone number. Instead of using your own picture, always use an **avatar**. Play it safe by avoiding web cam and voice chat features.

Playing on the Go

Many video games can be played using mobile apps. You can play some games by downloading them, or through social networks. Keep in mind that these games often start out as free, but they might ask you to pay if you want a prize or if you want to go to the next level. They also encourage you to ask friends to play.

Mobile apps make playing games easier when you're on the move.

Like any other video game, these games can distract you from the rest of your life. Be aware of how much you play and what information you share with the game and other users. Remember, the companies that make video games are trying to make a profit.

Security and Consequences

Whether you're playing games, texting, or just surfing the web, there are many dangers in the digital world.

Here are some ways to protect your devices:

- Update your **anti-virus software** and run regular checks.
- Keep your software up-to-date—updates from software makers often include security fixes.
- Be careful with your devices to avoid them being stolen or damaged.
- Make passwords long and strong and remember to change them often. Don't use easy-to-guess numbers or words such as your birthday or a pet's name.
- Learn to recognize spam and avoid opening messages from people or addresses you don't recognize.
- Use **parental controls**. Just as locking windows and doors at night keeps unwanted people out of your house, parental controls keep unwanted people out of your online world.

If you are careful, the Internet can be a great place to relax, work, and learn.

Think Before You Type

The key is to make good choices. Pay attention to the privacy settings on all your social media sites. Remember that nothing is truly private on the Internet. Never share personal information, such as your phone number or address, online—even with friends.

Don't give out real-time information about yourself on public networking sites. Never send or post images or videos you don't want shared with the whole world.

Don't ignore someone who is bullying you. Tell an adult right away. They can help you alert the website, the Internet service provider, special reporting centers, and even the police if necessary. Never delete anything. It's important to keep proof of the abusive or criminal behavior.

Have fun online, just do it safely.

Hot Topics
Q&A

What should I do if I meet a stranger online?

A: Not everyone you meet online is dangerous. Pay attention to what this person says and does. Talk about your new friend with other friends or an adult. If anything makes you uncomfortable, tell an adult you trust right away. Never give anyone you meet online information about where you live or go to school.

I've been doing things online that I shouldn't be doing, and something bad happened. I'm afraid I'll get in trouble. What should I do?

A: It might be difficult, but telling an adult you trust is the best option. Tell him or her what happened, when, and how. Then the adult can help you deal with the situation. And remember, don't delete the **evidence**.

What should I do if my parents or guardians take away my computer privileges or my phone? How do I regain their trust?

A: Be open and honest. If you are keeping secrets, the adults in your life may worry. Show them that you understand the risks.

Agree to take steps to be safe, like using parental controls and following time limits. Then the adults in your life will be more likely to trust you online.

My friend is always downloading movies and music for free, but my dad says it is against the law. Everybody does it. Is it really illegal?

A: Downloading files and sharing files is very popular. It's also okay. However, downloading music and movies without paying is against the law. The creator of the content can sue you in court. Or, the police might arrest you if the content is stolen.

A friend of mine is really good at using computers and is learning how to program. She said she can look at other people's computers. How can that be true?

A: Just like people can break into buildings and cars, some people learn ways to break into computers and computer networks. It takes special skills and practice. Some people, known as hackers, do this just for fun. But other people do it to commit crimes and cause mischief.

Breaking into computers is against the law no matter why you do it. You should tell your friend that what she does is very dangerous and unethical, like stealing or damaging other people's property. She could get into trouble, and so could you if you don't report her actions. Always remember that no computer or network is completely safe!

Other Resources

The following websites and helplines will provide you with trustworthy information about digital dangers.

In the United States

Internet Keep Safe Coalition (iKeepSafe)
www.ikeepsafe.org
This organization helps children learn to use technology safely.

Stay Safe Online
www.staysafeonline.org
Created by the National Cyber Security Alliance, this website provides information on how to stay safe online.

National Center for Missing & Exploited Children
www.cybertipline.com
You can use this site in the United States to report inappropriate content on the Internet or users that may be predators.

SafeKids.Com
www.safekids.com
Larry Magid started writing about Internet safety in 1994. His website SafeKids.com explores many parts of this topic.

Cyber Bully Hotline

www.cyberbullyhotline.com

1-800-420-1479

Use this site and helpline number to report cyber bullying, bullying, school violence, theft, cheating, drug abuse, sexting, and other problems at your school. You do not need to give your name. It also provides tips on how to deal with and seek out help on a range of problems.

In Canada

Canadian Media Awareness Network

www.bewebaware.ca

This is a national, bilingual public education program on Internet safety in Canada.

The Canadian Center for Child Protection

www.cybertip.ca

You can use this site in Canada to report inappropriate content on the Internet or users that may be predators.

Canada Safety Council: Online Safety Rules for Kids

canadasafetycouncil.org/child-safety/online-safety-rules-kids

The Canada Safety Council focuses on all types of safety issues for young people.

Kids Help Phone

www.kidshelpphone.ca

1-800-668-6868

You can call this number for a variety of issues, including those related to cyber bullying and other types of online problems. It's anonymous and confidential, and also staffed by professional counselors who speak English and French

Glossary

Note: Words appearing in boldface but not in the glossary have been explained in the text.

addictive Making people need something so badly they can't control themselves

anti-virus software Program that searches computer for malware and helps to remove it

avatar A computer icon that represents a person

catfish A person who lies about himself or herself online

computer virus A type of malware that is meant to damage computers and networks

cyber bullying Using digital devices and online services to harass a person

digital Technology or information that is electronic and computerized

download To copy information from the Internet on to a computer

evidence Information that shows something is true

feed A list or stream of posts in a social media account

hacker A person who can break into computer networks

handle A name or identifier for online communication

harassment Negative behavior towards a person

hoax Made-up story or practical joke

malware Software that damages or disables computers and computer systems

parental controls Features or settings that limit what a young person can do on an electronic device

phishing Tricking people into sharing financial information by pretending to be a real company

pornography Pictures or writings describing sexual behavior and intended to cause sexual excitement

predator A person who goes after other people to make them victims

program A set of instructions that can be carried out on a computer or digital device

reputation What people in general think about a person

sext A text or instant message that includes sexual material

sexually explicit When sexual acts or nudity are shown or described in detail

software Programs and other information used by a computer to make it work

spam Unwanted email sent to many addresses

wall The part of a Facebook profile where a person's posts appear

Index